Advice from a River

20 ❦ 16

Better World Press, Inc.
Oregon   Colorado   New Mexico

Published by Better World Press, Inc.
A Division of Your True Nature, Inc.
P.O. Box 272309, Fort Collins, Colorado 80527
800-992-4769 email: branch@yourtruenature.com
yourtruenature.com

©2005, 2016 Ilan Shamir   Advice from a River® is a registered trademark of Your True Nature, Inc.

No part of this book may be reproduced or transmitted in any form or by any means, electronic or mechanical, including photocopying, recording, or by any information storage and retrieval system, without permission in writing from the copyright holders.

Silk painting cover: Ilan Shamir
River woodcut illustrations: Chuck Black
Library of Congress Cataloging-in-Publication Data
ISBN 978-1-930175-30-3
　Shamir, Ilan, 1951-
　　　Advice from a River / Ilan Shamir
　　　1. Rivers
　　　2. Human Growth and Potential
　　　3. Nature
　　　4. Health and Wellness

Printed in the USA on recycled paper. Many thanks to the trees for their gift of paper! All paper used in the printing of this book has been replanted through the 100% Replanted program. Visit www.ReplantTrees.org.

The river, with its symphony of sounds, plays its soothing music. Here, the river shares its clear and timely wisdom about the flow of life – about living in harmony with nature and with ourselves.

It is so easy to get caught up in the rush of life. To forget the beauty and simplicity of nature. There are those days when it feels like we are fighting the current, swimming upstream, and longing for the simplicity of life.

I stand beside the river, watching the light playfully dancing over the moving water. I am soothed as a symphony of sounds fills the air. Seeing the rocks become rounded and smoothed over time, I relax into the natural flow. I am reminded so simply and gracefully of my own true nature.

Advice from a River...

Dear Friend . . .

Go with the Flow!

Be Thoughtful of Those Downstream

Slow Down and Meander

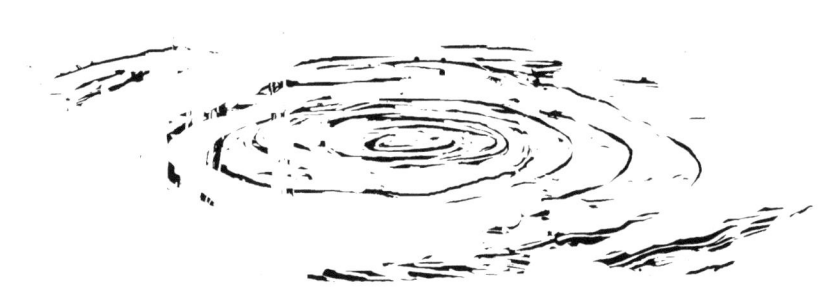

Be Clear

Follow the Path of Least Resistance for Rapid Success

Immerse Yourself in Nature:

Trickling Streams,

Roaring Waterfalls,

Sparkles of Light Dancing on Water

Delight in
Life's
Adventures
Around Every
Bend

Let Difficulties Stream Away

Live Simply
and Gracefully
in Your Own
True Nature . . .

Moving

Flowing

Allowing

Serene and on Course

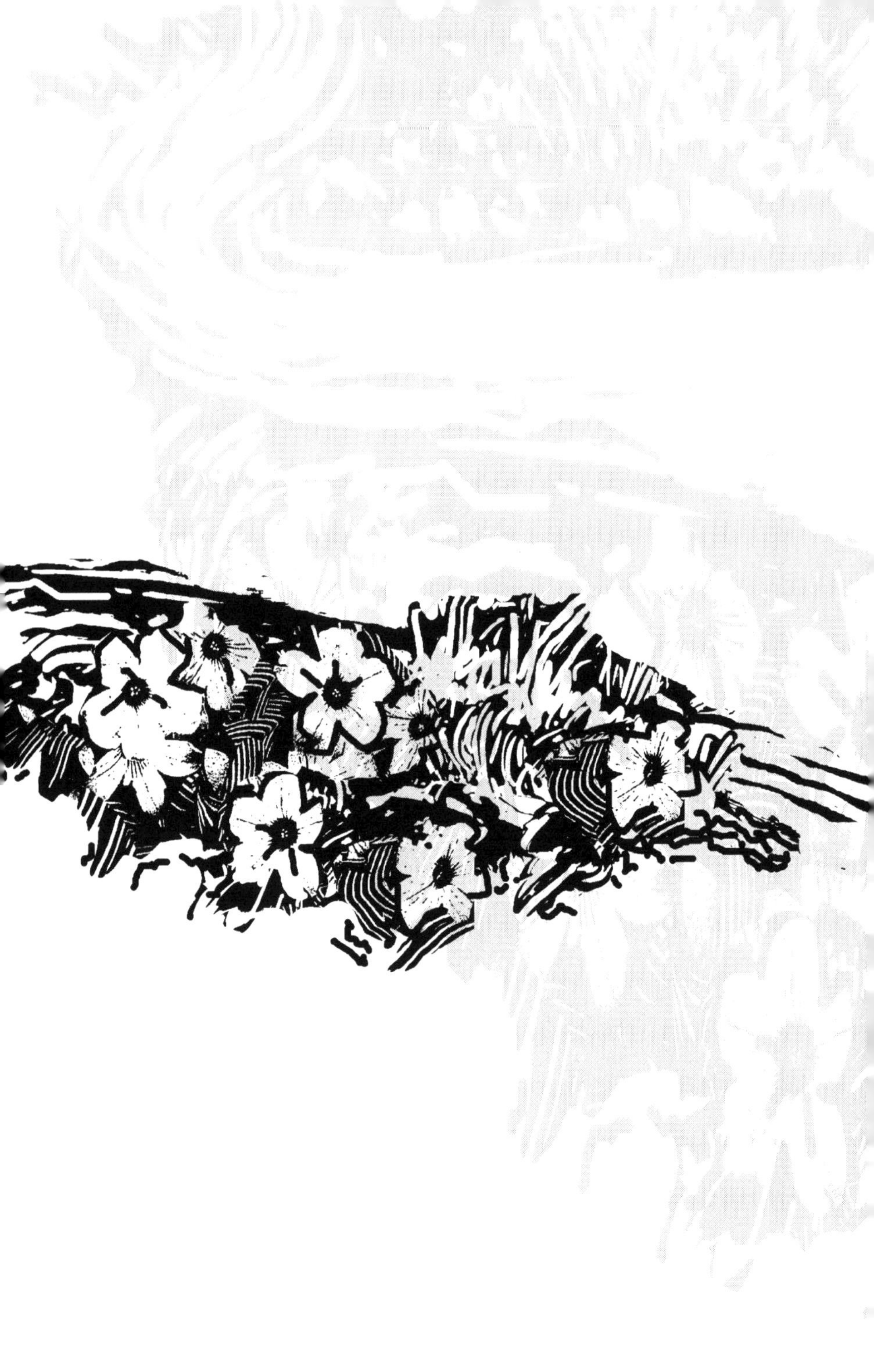

Rough Waters Become Smooth

If You Find
Yourself
Babbling

... Just Smile!

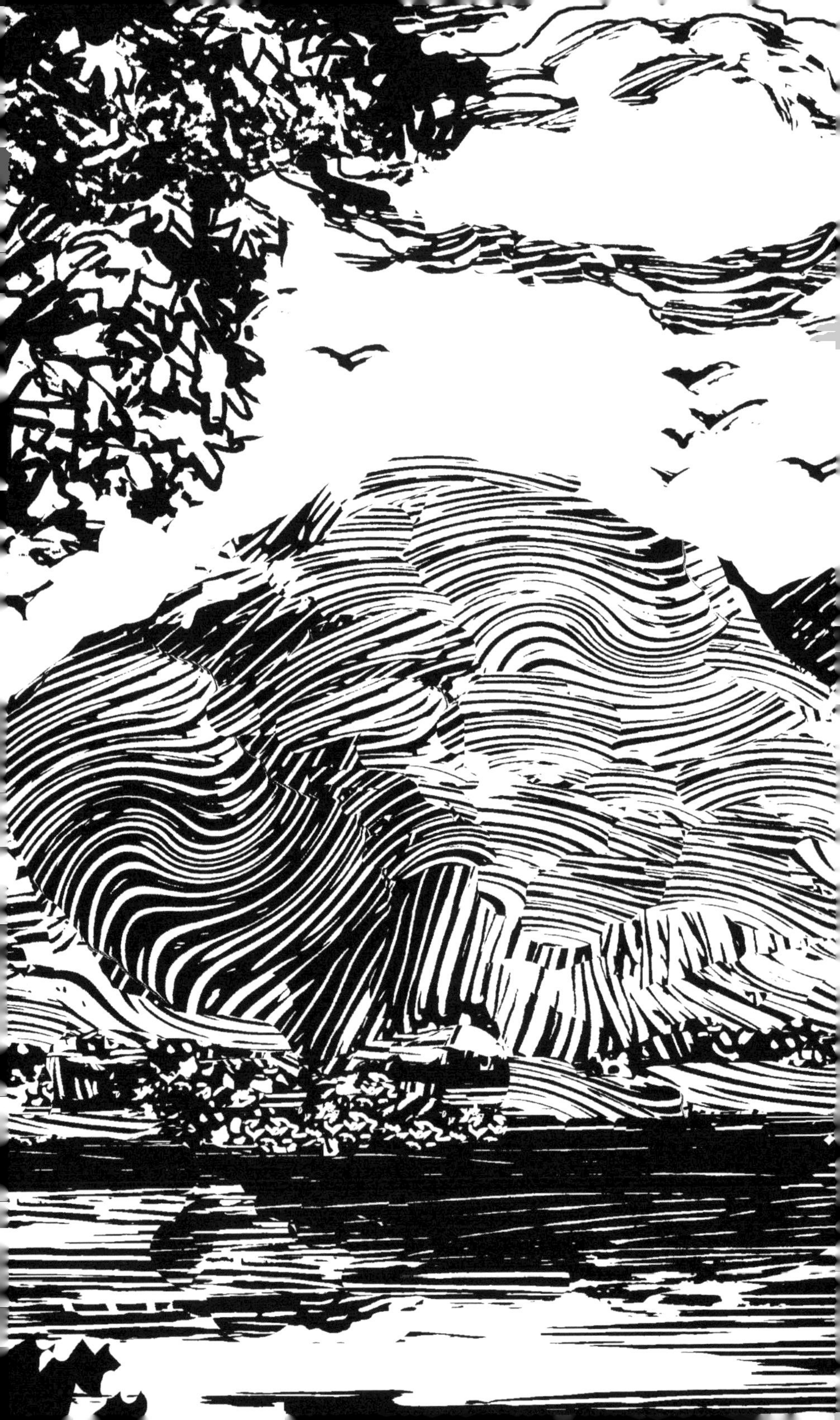

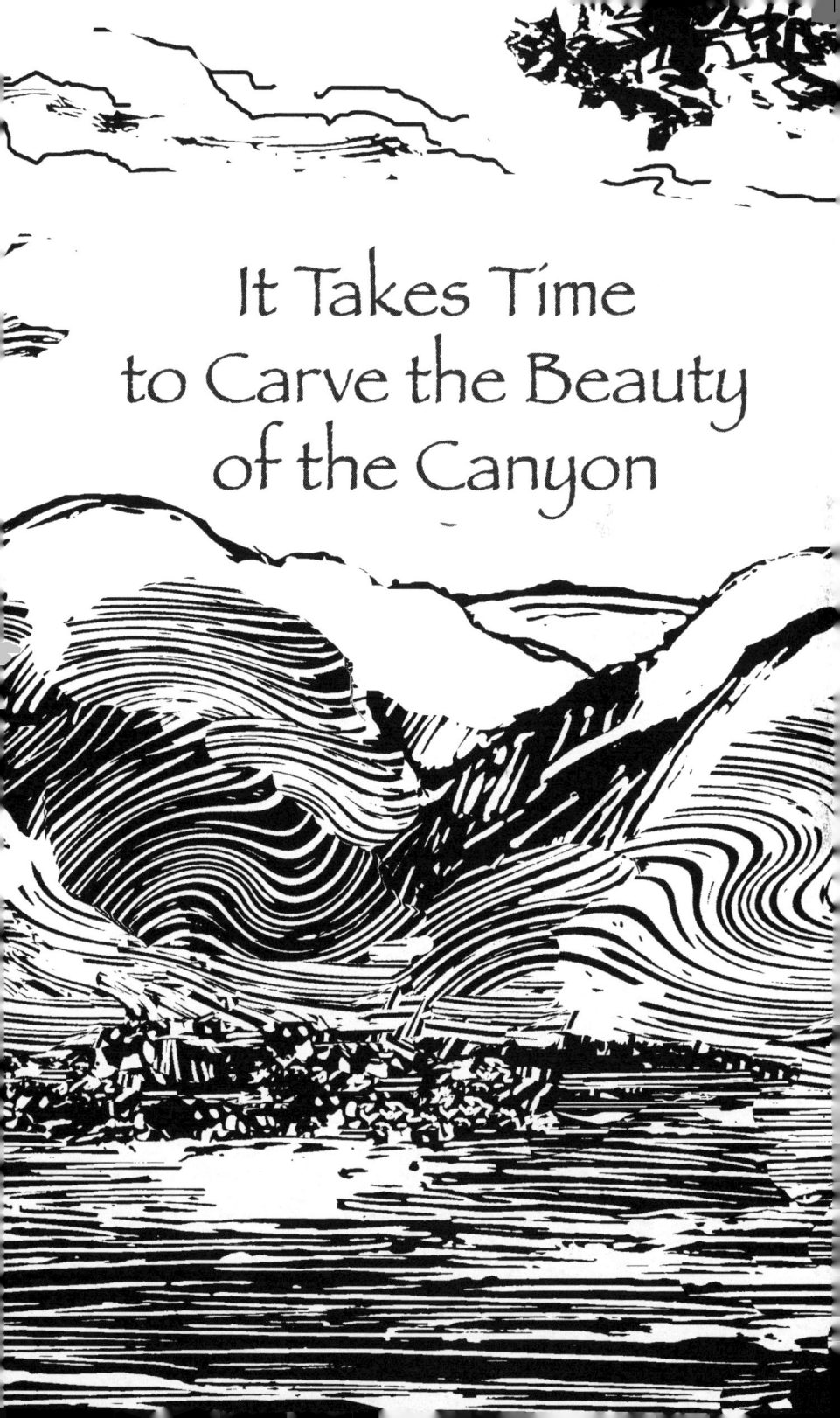

It Takes Time to Carve the Beauty of the Canyon

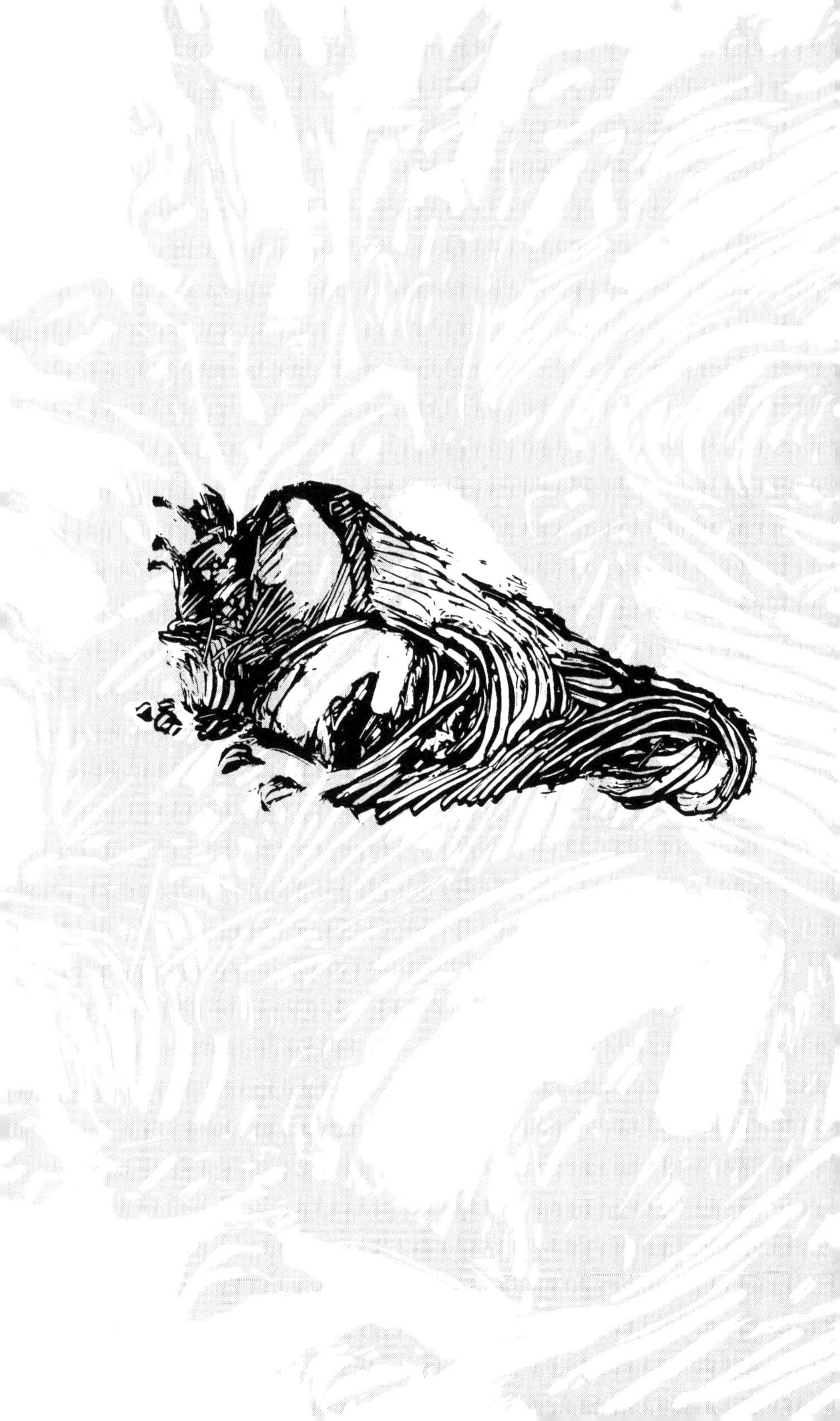

Go Around the Obstacles

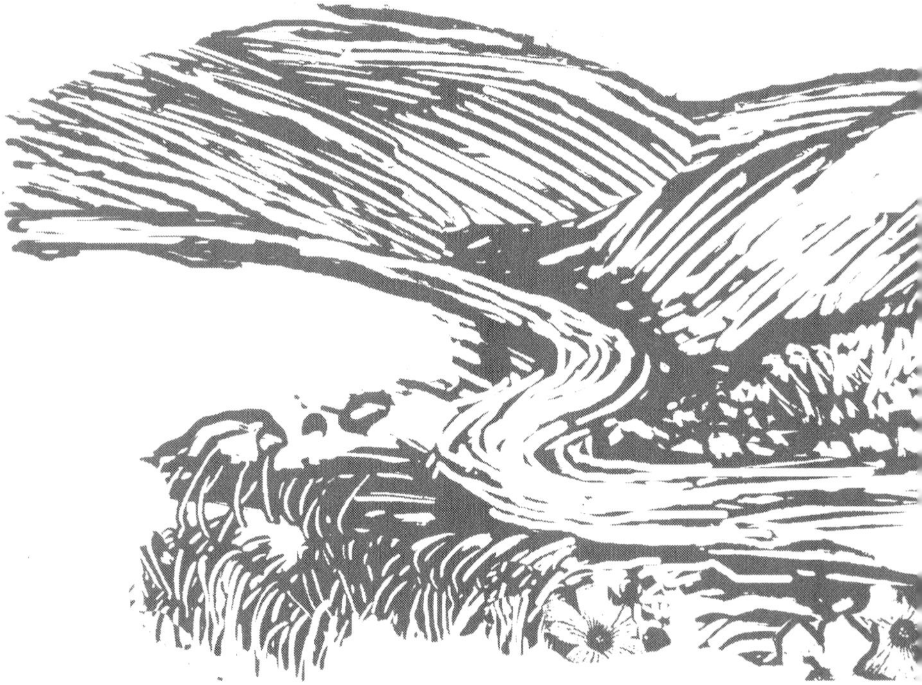

Stay

Current

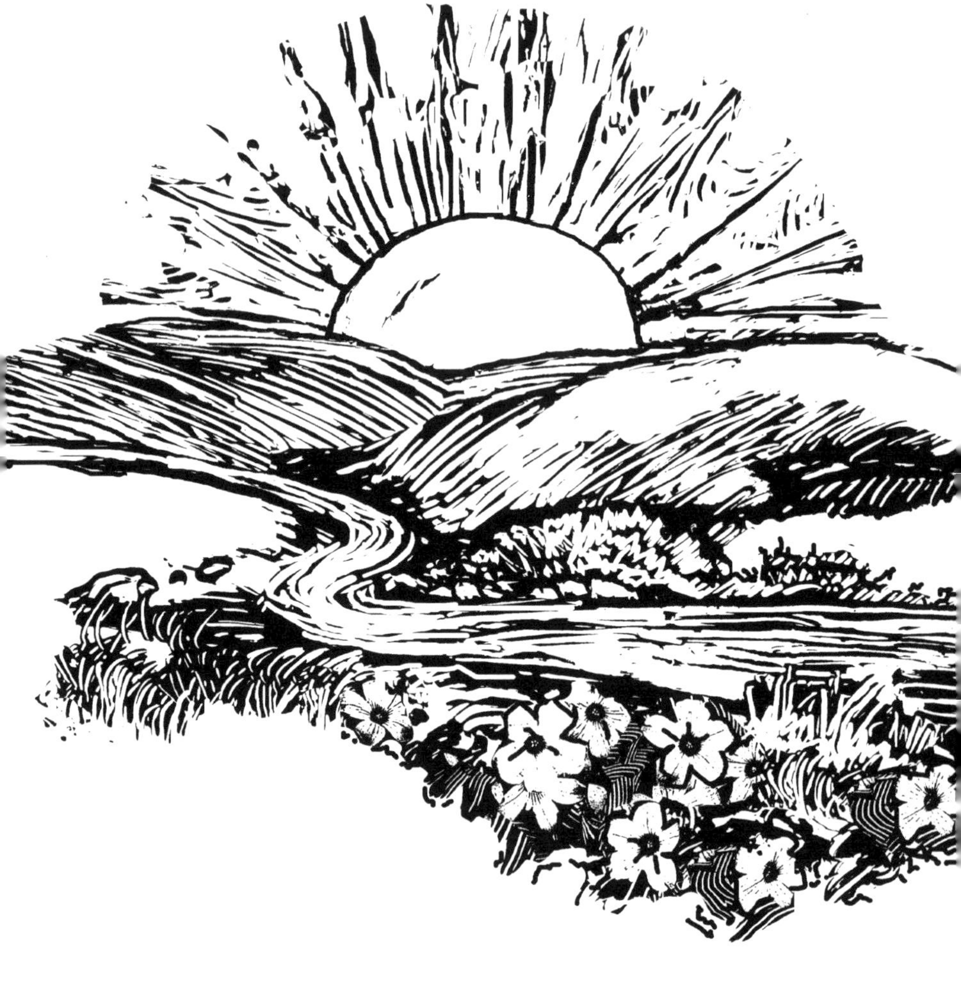

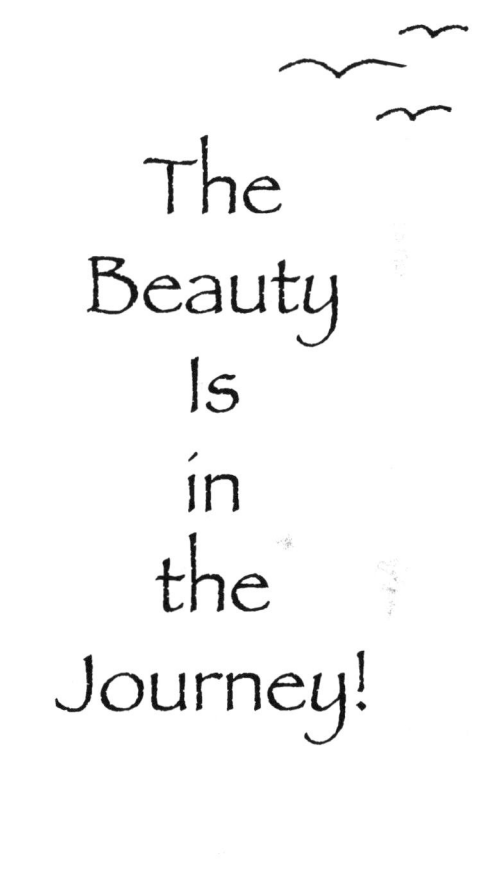

The
Beauty
Is
in
the
Journey!

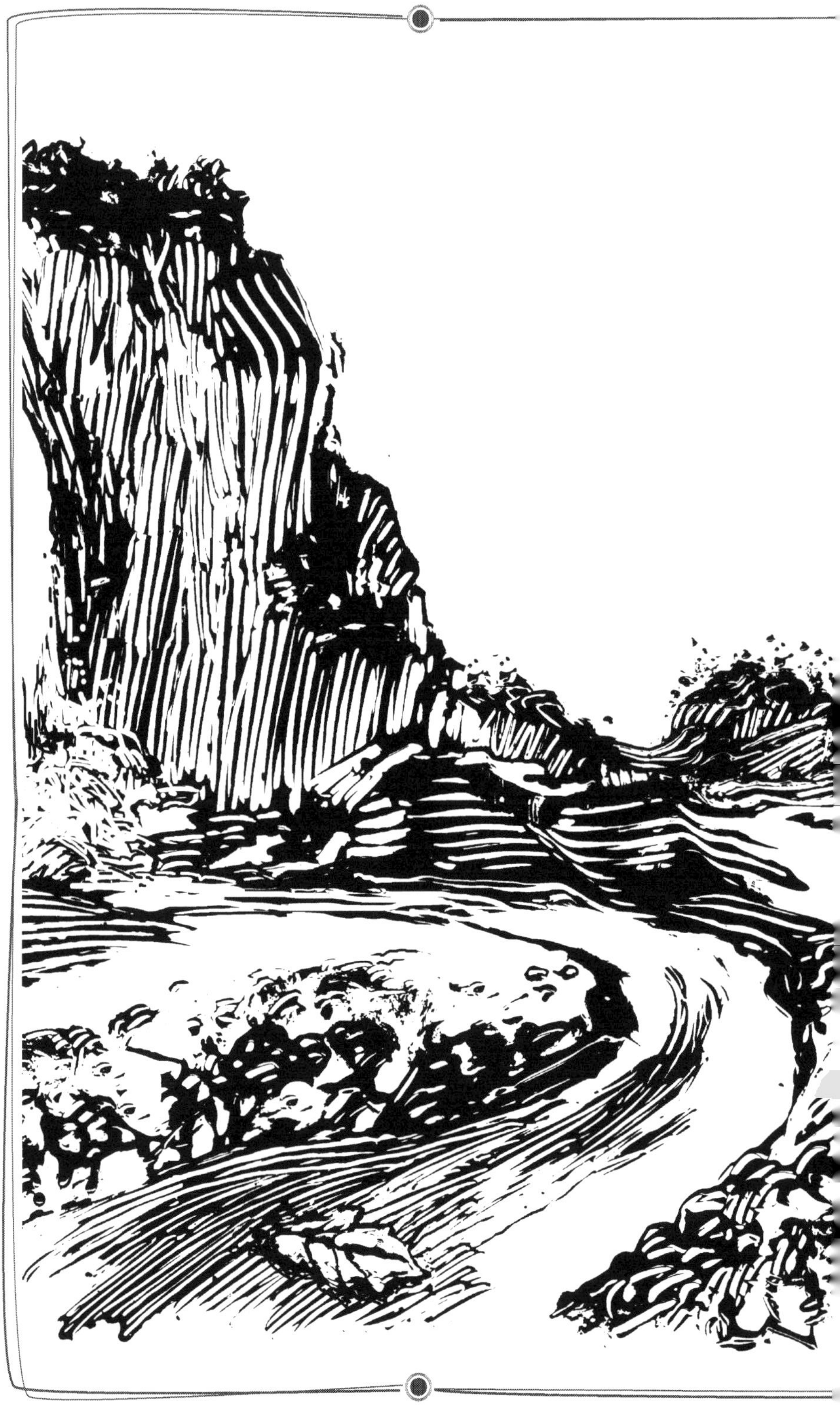

Advice from a River

Dear Friend . . .

Go with the flow!

Be thoughtful of those downstream

Slow down and meander

Be clear

Follow the path of least resistance for rapid success

Immerse yourself in nature:
  Trickling streams,
  Roaring waterfalls,
  Sparkles of light dancing on water

Delight in life's adventures
around every bend

Let difficulties stream away

Live simply and gracefully in
your own true nature . . .
    Moving
    Flowing
    Allowing
Serene and on course

Rough waters become smooth

If you find yourself babbling . . .
just smile!

It takes time to carve
the beauty of the canyon

Go around the obstacles

Stay current

    The beauty is in
        the journey!

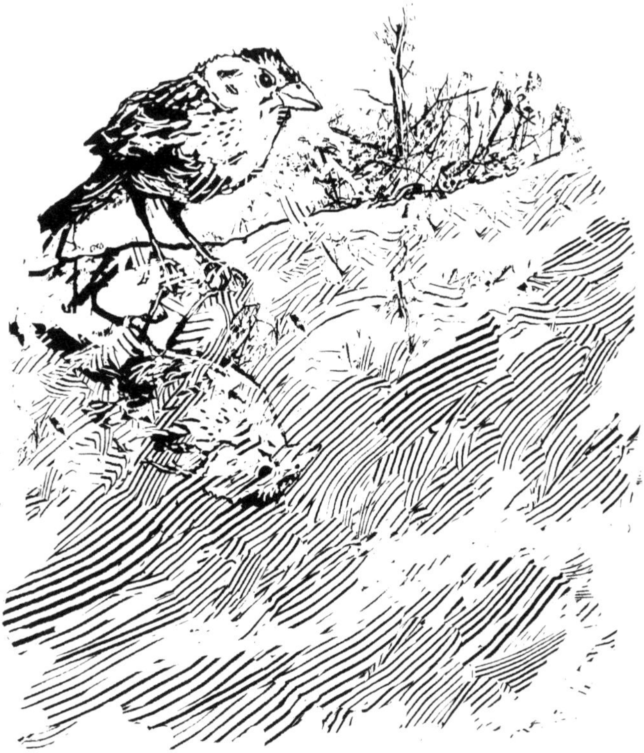

Caring for
the Earth

Rivers invite us to reconnect with the stream of life, the wisdom of nature, and our own well-being. The river itself guides us to . . . *Go with the flow . . . slow down and meander . . . and delight in life's adventures around every bend.* How could I not be filled with gratitude for the earth that has so generously given its gifts to me? For the life-sustaining water of streams, rivers, lakes, oceans, rain, ice, snow, fog, in its many forms of beauty.

So many have worked to protect and conserve the earth. Committed individuals such as David Brower, Steve Harris, Andrew Purkey, Jan Goldman-Carter, Casi Callaway, Stephen Mather, and millions of others have given back to the earth in their unique ways that will impact generations to come. The Aboriginal Australians have a fascinating way of stewarding the earth. Early in life, each villager is assigned a part of nature, their "Yuri," to watch and care for. One villager is responsible for the sea turtles, another for the whales, another for a certain species of bird, another for the nearby streams, and so on. The stewards tune into the health of "their" resource. If the village is concerned about the animal or has a desire to harvest, the steward is asked to speak on behalf of the animal, with the final word on what care might be needed or whether hunting will be allowed. If the species is thriving, hunting will be allowed. If the species is in peril, hunting is denied. Rather than compelling each villager to watch over all parts of nature, the village manageably divides and focuses the care.

The more we honor and celebrate the earth, the more we become active stewards. The earth offers amazing inspiration for our creative expression. Write a poem or a song about the sky, plant a garden, photograph wild birds, hike to a mountain lake, dance around a bonfire, write in your journal beside your favorite river. There are thousands of ways to express your love of nature.

The earth we live on, with its beautiful animals, flowing rivers, blossoming flowers, breathtaking sunsets, and exquisite landscapes, is precious. The closer I get to rivers, the more I am immersed in nature, rather than the city

I live in. I thrill to hear the sound of the water washing over the rocks, tickling the grasses as it passes by. The smells of water draw me closer to see the sparkles of sunlight dancing on the moving water. I kneel down on the banks of the river, scooping up water with my hands. I splash it over me and let out a big sigh of relief as I let it wash away my cares. The wind and cool fresh air soothe me and help me appreciate how beautiful it all is.

The river calls me to think about how I can give back, how I can be a better steward of the treasures of nature. There are so many great organizations that are working hard to care for the earth. It is simply a matter of choosing which ones to support. It's easy to assume that other people will keep these organizations alive, but if each of us does our small part by donating money or time, they will succeed in their work to restore healthy environments for all of us.

YourTrueNature.com has "learning links" that correspond to our Advice products. Choose your favorite river, lake, tree, animal, landscape, or habitat and find out how you can help it thrive. The site also features a wonderful, free Nature Curriculum for teachers and parents to encourage in children a love of the natural world. The curriculum's activities include art, writing, music, performance, celebrations, stewardship actions, and much more.

I remember playing in a small creek when I was growing up. It was alive, teeming with tadpoles, minnows, water bugs, tiny fish, algae, frogs, and so much more. Standing in the creek with water up to my knees, I was part of it all and feeling so playfully aware. This gift from the natural world was ever-changing and always full of surprises. It guided and shaped my connection to the earth, and in return for its companionship, I would care for the waters with my words, participate in river and lake cleanup days, use water wisely, and support organizations protecting this precious resource.

Living Your True Nature

What is our purpose, and how do we find it? It's easy to become so preoccupied with making a living that we forget to really live. When we live our true nature, we are called to discover what gives meaning to our lives, to go beyond ourselves in service to others, to live in harmony with nature, to express our uniqueness, and to realize our dreams.

Remember to take time to get close to the earth and its many moving waters–mighty rivers, sparkling forest streams, and winding creeks. As you sit near a river or lake, let your imagination drift and allow its wisdom to trickle in and comfort you. Let the natural flow of the water move and inspire you to find the flow of your own true nature.

We humans have common hopes, desires, and needs, but our special mix of talents, experience, geography, and timing makes our life's path absolutely unique. Not only will the rivers guide each of us to find and live our true nature, but so will the trees, mountains, skies, animals, and plants. We simply need to slow down, release our distractions, and be open to patient listening.

The journey to finding my own life's purpose, and creating work aligned with that purpose, was not easy. I found my time in nature so essential. The gentle winds soothed me; the rivers guided me to wash away my doubts and fears; the trees helped me remember my roots and branch out and grow. The star-filled skies reminded me of my smallness in the vast universe. Nature invited me to live my true nature. Eventually I would come to realize that my true nature was to use my creative gifts of art and writing to celebrate the natural world and encourage others to discover and share their beautiful and unique gifts. It has indeed been a blessing to find my true path.

Today, to stay aligned with my sense of purpose, I ask myself these ten questions: Am I living with intention and directing my life—or am I controlled by outside factors? Is there a flow to life, or does it seem like I'm swimming upriver? Am I expressing my unique gifts and talents? Am I caring for the earth and giving back in gratitude for its abundance? Am I finding and living my joy and also serving others? Am I open to receiving the wisdom of others?

Am I living a life of trust, clarity, alignment, and peace? Am I facing life's challenges and using them to grow, change, evolve, and become? Do I question the way things are and have the courage to make things the way they could be? Am I allowing myself to be tamed—or am I keeping my wildness alive?

Living our true nature is not something we strive to achieve; rather, it's a constant path of awareness, discernment, willingness, and openness. It's a daily practice of seeing what each new day brings. Years ago, when I leaned against the gnarled, ridged bark of an old tree, I asked for help. *How can I live my life with purpose and give back for this incredible gift of life I have been given? I need your help. I need your advice.* The giant tree shared its wisdom with the words for Advice from a Tree. I listened and wrote them down. One by one, I created expressions of these beautiful and timely words—a postcard, bookmark, poster, book, and journal—so I could share them with others. The feedback I got was that they touched and guided others as they had guided me. In an ever-unfolding journey, those few words from the tree were the seeds that inspired Advice from a River and the growing family of over one hundred elements of nature.

To stay on track in living my true nature, I have incorporated these approaches into my life:

Practicing meditation: taking time to sit and release, breathe, and clear.

Journaling: a wonderful way to dialogue through words and pictures and capture the ideas that come to me. Sometimes while I'm journaling, poems flow through me.

Clarifying intentions: concise written statements of what I intend to do or how I intend to be. I often write my intentions in my journal.

Learning: seeking out mentors who can help me answer my big questions and guide my path.

Traveling: a chance to get away from my daily routine and take a breather. A time to ask questions and receive guidance, relax in nature, clarify my goals, and gain the perspective and clarity I need to make course corrections in my life.

These five thoughtful practices have helped me live my true nature, and to evolve and grow and support others in living their true nature.

    As the river says, the beauty
                is in the journey!

Your True Nature

Your true and amazing nature is to rise like the sun,
to greet each day with your absolute brilliance
and shine your light for others.
Your true nature is the mountain.
To rise above it all, reach for new heights,
make solid decisions, and always be uplifting.
Your true nature is the river.
To go with the flow, stay current,
and remember that the beauty is in the journey.
Your true nature is the garden.
To plant seeds of kindness, sow seeds of happiness,
cultivate lasting friendships, take thyme for yourself,
and always dew your best.
Your true nature is the tree.
To stand tall and proud, branch
out to your full potential,
stay rooted in love, and enjoy the view!
Your true nature is to reach and grow
so that one day you can look back, and with a smile,
know you have lived your life in a way
that makes you proud.

Other friends of
the river share
their advice . . .

Advice from a Great Blue Heron

Wade into life

Keep a keen lookout

Don't be afraid to get your feet wet

Be patient

Look below the surface

Enjoy a good reed

Go fish!

Advice from an Otter

Take time to play

Keep your whiskers clean

Cherish clean water

Be spontaneous

Stay active

Don't be afraid to get your feet wet

Be otterly amazing!

Advice from a Wetland

Make a splash

Take time to reflect

Listen to nature

Reed more

Be green

Don't get bogged down

What's the rush!

Advice from a Trout

Show your true colors

Be a good catch

Don't be lured by shiny objects

Scale back

Cherish clean water

Know when to keep
your mouth shut

Don't give up
without a fight!

Ilan Shamir's Advice Book Series

Advice from a Tree &
Accompanying Journal

Advice from a River &
Accompanying Journal

Advice from a Mountain &
Accompanying Journal

Advice from a Garden

Advice from Nature
(Includes Advice from a Sea Turtle,
Owl, Canyon and many more)

More Advice from Nature
(Includes Advice from a Moose,
Wildflower, Night Sky and many more)

Other Titles

Tree Celebrations-
Planting and Celebrating Trees

PoetTree-
The Wilderness I Am

Simple Wisdom-
A Thousand Things Went Right Today!

The True Nature of Designing and
Promoting Successful Products

The True Nature of Designing and
Promoting Successful Programs

My Colorado
Nuggets of Wit and Wisdom

Words

*We invite you to visit us at:
yourtruenature.com for hundreds of other items including collectable frameable art cards, bookmarks, posters, mugs, magnets, t-shirts and more.*

Journal Pages

Write about a river that is special to you . . .

The rivers flow not past,
but through us!

John Muir

Draw a picture of a river, paste a photo, or write a river poem...

For river and nature activities, visit:
yourtruenature.com/activities

Ilan's Special Thanks

To my river buddies Fred Boshardt and John Stapp for our long list of amazing adventures and surprises around every bend.

Thanks Rich Schrader for your gentle and knowing nature and your important river work here in Santa Fe and all of New Mexico. Each of the thousands of kids that you teach about the rivers may one day be a leader to carry on your important work. And for your awesome music and endearing friendship.

Much gratitude for all the splashy and fun water memories at summer camps I attended and for the opportunity to be a counselor at: Scotty's Ranch – Wimberly TX, Indian Creek and Bear Creek Scout Camps, TX, Camp Champions - Marble Falls Texas, Camp Thunderbird – Bemidji, MN, Farm and Wilderness – White River Junction VT,

I feel so blessed for all of the rivers I have explored and loved . . . San Antonio, Pedernales, Llano, Frio, Guadalupe, Grand Ronde, Deschutes, Poudre, Big Thompson, Rio Caliente, Current, Jacks Fork, Gullfoss, Dettifoss, Aare, the Rhone and hundreds more.

Deep gratitude to the awesome, amazing team at Your True Nature, Inc. - Special thanks to Patti, Allison, and Jill for staying current and keeping up with the constant flow of orders, even when they flood in!

Thanks Jasmine Quinsier for your bringing your graphics, talents and smiles to help package our Advice Series. Kristen Barendsen for finding things that no other copy editor could possibly find. A great big thanks to you, Stella Togo - my book writing and marketing coach for your finishing touches that made this body of work come together with style.

Keynote programs
Breakouts
Workshops

Through the simplicity and beauty of trees and nature, Ilan Shamir calls us to branch out, grow, and celebrate our true nature! Author of the bestselling Advice from a Tree products and "A Thousand Things Went Right Today," Ilan's inspiring programs are a perfect addition to conferences and events.

Member of the:
*National Associaton for Interpretation
*National Speakers Association Colorado
*National Storytellers Network

YOUR TRUE NATURE®
Grow Up!

yourtruenature.com

Have a Tree Planted for Someone Special!

Your purchase price of $8.95 for one tree, or $18.95 for a three-tree grove, plants and cares for native trees in projects in El Salvador, Honduras, Costa Rica, and Nicaragua through the nonprofit organization Trees, Water & People. The recipient gets a beautiful personalized greeting card from you, and both you and the recipient can visit the planting area online!

A simple gift that lasts a lifetime!
It's as easy as 1, 2, TREE...

Qty ($8.95)   Qty ($18.95)   Occasion

___   ___   All Occasion

(Friendship, birthday, Mother's Day, thank you, birth, anniversary, congratulations, Father's Day, wedding, graduation)

___   Holiday
___   Memorial

Your Name _____
Address _____
City/State/ZIP _____
Email _____
Telephone _____

Total Qty ____ at $ 8.95 = $_____
Total Qty ____ at $18.95 = $_____
Shipping $____6.50____
GRAND TOTAL $_____

Send with your check to:
Your True Nature, Inc. Box 272309
Fort Collins, CO 80527, (970)282-1620
Email: orders@yourtruenature.com

Visit our website for more information or to order online at yourtruenature.com